D1827800

ELEMENTAL

Clarence C. Bess

Featuring Photography by :
Rogerio Bussad

Elemental

Copyright © 2017 Clarence C. Bess
All rights reserved. Printed in the United States of America. No part of this book may be used or reproduced in any manner whatsoever without written permission except in the case of brief quotations embodied in critical articles or reviews. For information, address Clarence C. Bess 75 Ocean Ave. Suite 5K Brooklyn, NY 11225 / sheikra75@yahoo.com or http://clarencecbessactualityaskew.blogspot.com

NOTICE TO READER : This book contains images and language intended to be displayed, viewed, shared, and/or read by mature audiences only. Your possession of this book and its contents releases the author, artist, publisher, and all other entities associated with it from any and all liability arising from such possession.

Book Design & Editing by Clarence C. Bess
Photography by Rogerio Bussad /
© 2016 Rogerio Bussad & Clarence C. Bess

**Photography by Mick Andreano / Used With Permission

Bess, Clarence C., 1976-
Bussad, Rogerio, 1967-

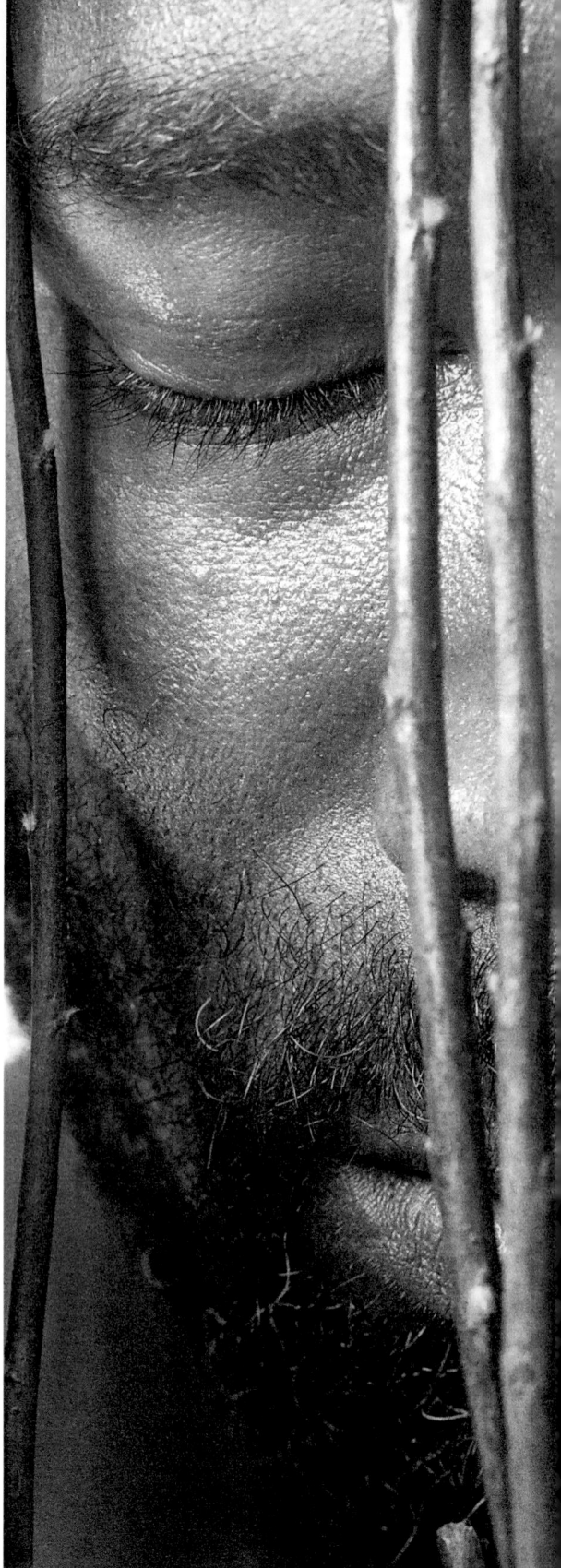

-Visual Selections-

Conceptual Designs & Costumes by C.C. Bess
Digital Editing by R. Bussad
*Body art by T. Stacheki
+Body art by C. C. Bess, G. Kleinman,
& R. Bussad
#Hair by G. Kleinman

With profound gratitude,
This book is dedicated to

C. Adams-Martin

For giving me the songs

&

D. Bowers

For giving me the words

Together you gave me inspiration.
Together you gave me a voice.

A very special thanks to

Rogerio Bussad

For joining me along this artistic journey.
Your talent is profound.

Timothy Stachecki & Garry Kleinman

For bringing the elements to chromatic life.

Also to
Akili "AC Wordslinger" Carter
Thank you for your support.

-Foreword -
Through the Fire : On 'Elemental'

The term that comes to mind is avant-garde.
Always on the cutting edge, 'Elemental' brings a refreshing and thought-provoking voice to the universal song of poetry.
Partnered with Bussad's visionary statements, their journey fluidly unfolds.

"The most powerful weapon on earth is the human soul on fire." ~ Ferdinand Foch

With the following collection,
we witness these souls forever engulfed in the flame of creation,
their pieces reflecting that heat.
Having had the honor of performing Clarence's poems, 'Elemental' reiterates his body of work. His approach here seamlessly embodies organic yet practiced eloquence in keeping his pen on the pulse of society. Together with Rogerio, a relationship unfolds burning their interpretations, universal truths even, into the subsequent pages embarking the reader on a tour-de-force from the bowels to the heavens of existence.

"I went to that place on the borders of thought and relevance." ~ Clarence C. Bess

It's as if they are pushing the edges of the reader's mind.
Forcing a return to understanding the primal side of creation. Elemental also highlights the eternal struggle all artist experience; The battle between intrinsic and extrinsic motivations and inspirations. One in the same, these words and images allowed me to become a part of this creation, a living breathing poem in many ways.

'Elemental' is a total mental, physical, and emotional experience,
embodying that true purpose of poetry.

- Akili Carter -

-Elemental-

This morning,
There was light
And a sharp chill caressing me beneath warm thoughts of you blanketing me.
This morning,
The leaves were still
Mother's breath did not rattle them, and I strained to hear what chorus I could.
This morning,
My voice is parched
Devoid of its tone, robbed of its cadence, it bides time to heal knowing it shall
come forward again... soon.
This morning,
The very ground beneath my feet rejects me sending miniature waves of
lightning through my heels with each step.
Everything in this world about me is muted.
Though light breaks horizon, yells triumphantly through clouds seeking to
gather, I'm breaking down; losing my elements beneath this chrysalis muting
my world until I can break free...
To fly.

-EARTH-

'The poetry of the Earth is never dead'
-John Keats-

-Mother-

Eternal
Born of thee
In unison we breathe;
And I wonder, beholding you,
What hopes and dreams you held for we
When you brought us to the shore
From creation's great sea.

-To the Bone-

Winter won't leave my bones
Despite rainbow blossoms
And scents to follow.
Won't leave my script
Remains bleeding from my pen
An open wound left to fester in the approaching heat
Of change.
My shades refuse to rise.
Ebony infinity holds me.
Echoes me into a submission only faith could rival
Despite promises of better days relentlessly bombarding
Breaking through to cast hazy shadows of hope
Around those loosened parts of me
Worn from my now ancient attempts to greet heaven
In this ongoing hell I was taught to seek respite from.
Winter won't leave my bones
Won't divorce me,
Release me,
Allow me to thaw in all my dreams
Dancing just beyond my mind's cells;
Won't sing the final chorus
Connect the final phrase
And leaves me as incomplete as...

-Turtle-

Turtle hangs his ancient head low
Parts with memories
He can no longer carry beneath his shell
Now as dusty as the years which have passed
Aging him,
Bowing him,
Confining him,
Though I believe personally,
To stare upon the road.
Periodically
His head rises
Catching glimpses of the now people;
He turns facing outwardly to watch the cityscape pass
And I am left to wonder his manicure
And story of his somehow
Intentional unkemptness.
Turtle I've named him,
The arch of his spine
Alcohol?
Drugs?
Age?
Life I figure
Hard and purposeful;
This is the consequence biological and otherwise.
Is that me there beneath his blackened nails?
At the ends of his silvering hair?
He moves forward
Aware of the stops
Recognizing yet bowed.
I wonder his God...
Is this me?
Is this me?

-Release-

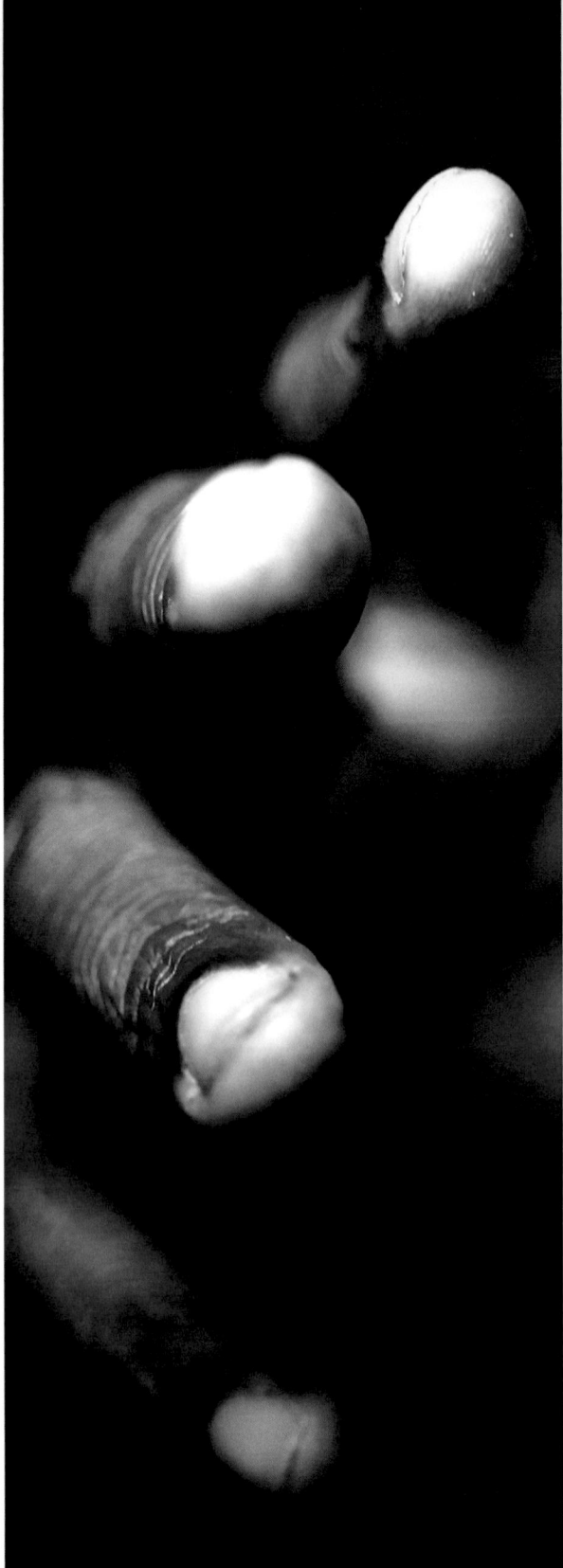

Complex goodbyes
He exits with delicate deliberate moves
Ducking behind the column
To wave a last farewell.
She stutters in her age
Nervously offering reciprocation
As time is winning
From her heels to her hands
Further still to her face
She smiles now alone
Thinking of this possible last chance
Last dance for love.
I wonder them
I, we in the schemes
And trappings of this need
Despite gravity
Of situation and flesh.
I go back to his eyes
His contorted visage
And how beautiful it became
As that moment unfolded
And he hid there only for her,
For them,
For that elongated departure
And the fact that he was just as surprised
There could be any interest.
I knew this watching
Observing one of the finer points of existence
They looked like first timers,
Or was it long-time-since'rs?
Regardless, They bring color vivid
To my otherwise monotone palate
As he finally makes his way up the station
stairs
A nervous twitch in his spine;
His body and heart
Longing to steal just one more glance
And she now snuggling eyes-closed
In the memories of a touch
And the playful games
One who's in love
Can never tire of playing...

-Pretty In Pink-

Dissolved and spent
She fumbled through bag upon bag
Tossing and folding
The collection of her tome.
An obvious hard road
Full of cheeseburger blow-jobs,
Five dollar hand-jobs,
And too many promises to the pusher-man
To make payment next time
'Lest she swore
Her overused dried split could be his for the taking.
She continued in that place
Tucked away from most people's sight
In that late hour
As they ate and conversed
About the night's drunken escapades
Ignoring her just as they should
Except for the eyes ever watchful
Taking in her wasted self
As she did up her knotted hair
In a failed attempt at beauty.
With this she turned
Catching glimpse of my prying eyes;
I cringed at the sight of her sunken cheeks
And hands whose skin appeared tissue paper thin
Revealing what little life she had left
Frantically moving about,
A caged animal looking for escape.
I cringed
Because this was not age
Not natural
But an oddly admirable asphalt wisdom
Earned in alleyways,
Parked cars,
And other places untold
But well known in stories
Countless women told
In hushed conversations
As warnings to the youth
They sought to influence.

-Nappy-

Wound so
Tight
Soft to
Touch
He was nappy
Ragged
This way and
That
Way which makes the girls
Want to grow up a little quicker
Past their bloomers
To their French-cuts
French nails
French kisses
Hershey style
He was nappy
So tight
So
Together
Fellas
Wanted to kick it
Lick it
Stick
It;
That vibe,
His swagger
Get involved
In whatever he was after
Whether it was
Uncut
Straight up
Down low
Just so

He looked nappy
But he was soft
To the touch
Sweet to the lips
Dark chocolate
90% cocoa
Bitter
Sweet that is;
Always out
For the boys and girls
Rotting teeth
Adding inches to the seams
Playing the field
Between wedding bells
And hoop dreams
Caught in the conundrum
Of privacy
French cuts
French kisses
And who should partake of these
treasures...

-Lower-

Beneath
Me
Subconsciously released
Refusing
to let the ground beneath
Complete
This horizon rotating me
Until I think
That I am standing still.
Sun setting over me
You smile
And parts underneath growl
Hunger to feast
Enveloping
this need complete;
Lower me
To solitude and simple tune
In tune with amethyst vision
As twilight
Plays with night's tears
Shimmering
Distant in that complexity
Lower me
Underneath
Bring me into nascency
Birth forth
Burst forth
From underneath
The earth between and those
dreams waltzing
Through time's obsidian sheen.

-Descend-

I hate going to work this way.
The path always seems to be descending
Further down into the bowels of this place;
The corner of the bathroom
Just behind the toilet
Where the cleaner can never seem to reach.
This is behind the stove
On top of the cupboards
Faces caked with a monstrous survival
But deft understanding
Or is it understatement
We are all thinking the same
Out here
On our way
Into the hush-hush problems
And the hoping
We don't have to duck a stray killer.
I hate going this way
Downward
Too close to buildings
Which even modern
Appear ramshackle;
Loathe my foreign existence
Not seeing or feeling my tribe move about me
I am caught in the survival of this place
These mornings
And the rumble, rumble of my head
Along these tracks
As I move one stop further into oblivion…

-Eight Inches-

Winter lays its bitter lips upon my flesh
Again
Crystallizes my blood
Until shards disintegrate me from the inside out.
I huddle in my conscience
Warmer with dreams of flight
And a blue veil of clarity which seems lacking now
Here in nature's steel,
Unmoving and brutal.
I long for the sun's love
Think on past frolics within its rays
Naive ejaculations of achievement and conquering
When alas,
I was the one being conquered.
Long to feel again
Like everything was virgin
Untouched by the sheltered me
Just ripe and waiting to let their nectarous juices flow
Stain my fingers
As they grasp frantically
Because this time,
I know the importance of their sustenance
And I cannot,
Will not get enough from their groves
Because I haven't all the time
And I know this all too well.
Winter laid it's bitter lips
Gave me a sweet dream of my every-things
Every-wheres;
Left me to huddle
Counting down the days...

-Funky Underground-

The big one
Barry White beard
Plucked his lady gentle
While the young one
Made true those dreams
As he sat in class
No. 2's in either hand
Drumming out the sounds
That pave the way to coolness
Women's secret places
And enough free drinks
To make a belly proud.
Keyboards light
Almost lost
In the over-bassed reverberations
Of this tiny place
With this tiny band
Making a gargantuan sound of ecstasy
Which laid down
Smooth and deliberate memories
Of a time
When all I wished for
Was a set of parents
Who cursed a bit
Drank a little
And danced in a way
That would make church ladies whisper
But would keep them young
And make me proud at some point to say,
They lived
Providing a sense of reality, balance.

Members came and went
Along a tour through the ages
Of sound
Moving from simplistic
Universal beats
To complicated matters of the heart
And all those polyester snapshots
Everyone smiling
Because we at the time
Were closer to possibility
And moving on up
To our deluxe forty acres
Underneath the the sky-eye-eye
Despite a cancer that grew among us
To destroy us;
Then again
Maybe that's just evolution inevitable...
For the moment though,
I couldn't care
Transported on this added violin
Taking me down home
Even amongst the urban of this place;
Saw their eyes roll back
The pure fulfillment of competence
As B-B's look-alike
Caressed his Lucille
Climaxing her,
Not to mention a few ladies in the crowd
Now
Upon it's feet
Undulating
An ocean of worshipers
In this house of blue funk
Watching these disciples
Break the bread of truth
Drink the spirit of time
At least for music
So many wish to return to;
Live,
Beyond studio confines
There where it joins with the masses
Simultaneously building
And tearing down
The houses of our being...

-Next to Nothing-

Fatality
Very definition of these faces
Someone said are supposed to represent me;
Just whose dream am I in anyway?
The murk of their travesties sloshes beneath me
Finds it's way into the microscopic cracks in my soul
Tainting what minuscule hope I had in man;
His ability to manipulate God's elements
Only to have to beg his mercy in repentance.
Which god was it again that created me?
I have a lot of questions.
Too many questions in fact
Embedded in my prayers
Repeated each time I see their faces
Wondering why can't I choose to move on...
Beyond 1976 possibly?
At least that's what she said.
And of course there was truth there
Just as much as here
Just as much as there was lies
And carefully placed innuendo;
You, as it is with others, think me the fool.
Fatality.
Fatalistic my strides
As I maneuver between who I am and what I am not
Hoping to attain a casual enough gait
Avoiding suspicion and the ever-present reprimand
Of being made the example of the architect's power...
I think it's about time for a personal uprising.
I am that which is everything as much as it is nothing;
That faint wonder witnessed just when there's a perfect culmination
Of shadow and thought;
That which dissipates only to return.
Universal.
Unanswerable.

-Inevitable-

Instantaneous was the return
To just after buildings fell
So fresh,
Reasoning at best was circumspect
And the body count kept mounting.
We weren't as old
As grey and weary
And possibly sprang forward
With each drunken kiss;
You are the first
To bring memories forward
To have my gut do a time warp
Back to places virgin and bright.
You are that moment of clarity
I thought I'd never see
Here
As this place was not me
Until that very moment I saw your smile
And suddenly I was in the past
Standing there in the present
Of you feeling it too
As we briefly reminisced
While I became suddenly aware of the irony
That was the sapphire and tonic upon my breath
A shade of our favorite drink
I'd had too many of that night
Long ago
When solace and escape from the history
Which surrounded
Was found within your arms as we lay.
Instantly I understood
Now this place was me
Was home
As I would look to every corner
With a dry smile and bitter tear
As the echoes of my footfalls returned to me
With this and other meetings to come…

-Songstress-

Songstress Spring
Singing melody
Supple, subtle
Senses overrun
With the seduction
Of her waking
Slipping once again closer to me
Still lost and stumbling
Through Winter's sleep.

-Observations-

Looking now
Upon these two souls at play
Memories return
Innocent interaction;
Different days
Far more accessible and savvy these days
Truth at the tips of their fingers
I want to play fortune-teller
See how close I can get.
Now I find myself looking all the time
At these unfinished canvases
Wondering which colors will adorn
And will motifs lend themselves classic
Or modern
Now I observe
Find myself wondering
Was my own future so obvious
In someone's eyes?
Did someone read me
Paint me
Here in my present state
Or was I left out to the rains
To be muddled?
A modern mistake
My creator couldn't bother to finish
Because even the discarded have a place
In the collection of existence.

-36 Blossoms-

Lest these blooms disperse
Beyond this forest
Their beauty echoing before them,
I fear the keeper's wrath.
Stubbornness abound
Too late to liberate them
From the rampant recidivism of their flesh,
They'll wither
Collect at the base of subsistence
And be gathered
To perpetrate their master's plan.
Lest theses blooms are tended
The disentanglement of their bouquet
From these brambles set
Shall be brutal;
Premature deaths
The song of their screams billowing
Like sheets to a wind,
Stunning violence.
I witness 36 blossoms born.
36 blossoms grow,
Then 36 blossoms die.
All by the hands of their keeper.

-Spring Doe-

Reflection kisses itself
Looks across the divide to me
Innocence and wonder
As I become another lesson in his young world.
She pulls him closer
Comfort and warmth
Him crossing his legs just like her
And I am taken
Emulation
She is subtle in her words
And he in return
Tells his secret story barely above a whisper.
There is no phone in his hands
And his vocabulary is one of respect
He is already light years ahead
Because of love
And I suspect by the way she takes his hand
Guiding him off the train
He will remain with his doe eyes
For many years to come.
How striking it has become
To see the face of a child
Upon the face of a child.

-Forest-

I went to that place
On the borders of thought and relevance;
Watched my accord decay
Until all that was left
Was rebirth;
Lush and promising.

-AIR-

'The world is full of poetry. The air is living with its spirit…'
-James Gates Percival-

-Ah, Yes-

With that, satisfaction came
Lifted me to a place only God could conquer.
I thought him,
rolled him over my pallet
swallowed and,
'Yes'
Finality
Oneness
Taking-IN-ness
To a point of fulfillment
and a licking of lips-ness
like LL Cool J sexiness
Dreams
Wants.
With those,
Syllables
I punctuated myself to an end
To my structure
That
Now
This was possible
And I was officially a part
Of that exclusive club known as...
Palpitations
Dumbfoundness
Anticipation
and a wanting to never part
From those eyes
And the depths of the soul
Which lay beyond them;
With that,
I tumble again and again...

34

-Beat-

I love this place
These moments
Lost in the j's interpretation
Of what it is these masses
Us
The swarm want to feel.
This is elemental
Mental
Subliminal
This pounding as every bump
Works it's way deeper
against my cavity;
This is a truth
This place
And the souls gathered to release
Relate
With every ounce of everything
which flows
To
From
And beyond them
In this cosmic
Cataclysmic movement that is
The turntable
Beneath our creator's hands…

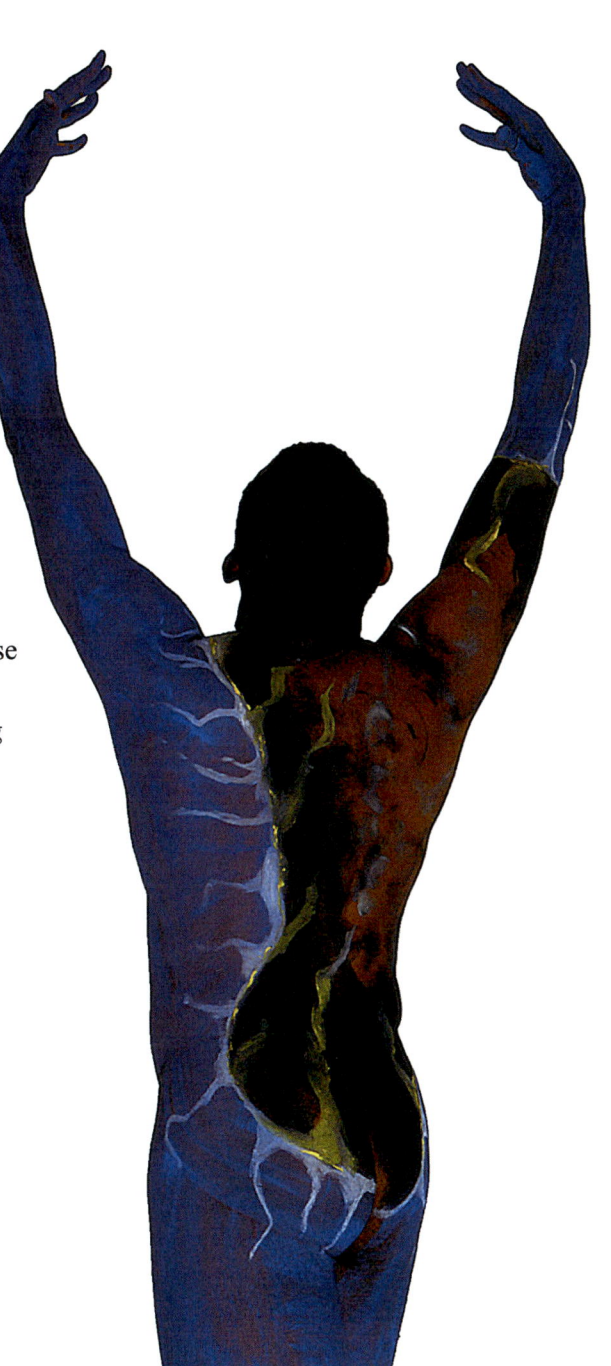

-The Singer-

Making his way
Up and down the aisles
Just he and his imagination
Honed
In the pursuit of happiness
Temporary.
Conversations abound
His melody cuts right through
To pockets
On to passing hands
Into his cap overturned
Slowly filling
With the cabbage
That never grows old.
His needle skips
(Several times)
Till his fingers snaps
Reverberating a time long-gone
But so desired
Till he jokes
Returning us
To the reality of his performance
He just needs a little extra change
For whatever is his urgency...

-Findmuck-

Ghost lay silent between life and love
And somewhere between my soul did appear
Lost within his eyes sallow
And the image of her head resting there
I saw beauty again in this place where
Souls come together at a quarter past twelve
Rocked to sleep by the rumble and sway
Of this dimension so bold
None of us could imagine another way.
His is the ghost
And I'd compromise for a chance to know that
truth
Foray into the depths of an unknown soul
Come again, my friend
You can't know an end
To lids which cover the proof;
So I rest within words I'll rehearse again
As I flee into my fervor of dreams
Sit back beneath the lights
Hold myself tight
Maybe when I awake everything will be
alright.

I found myself traveling down a dusty road
Of a memory I never thought too dear
Demons which I thought I'd let go
Their faces began to appear
Strange how the winds began to blow
As if God himself did hear
And to myself I thought
How could I ever forgive those souls
Who instilled all the heartache and fear?
Painful, the truths revealed with time
As the veils of youth begin to ascend
Shameful the fools whom convinced
themselves
They've nothing to do with the sin
And ghost lay somewhere between these
parallels
Stretched out before me for years;
Why did I have to run so far away?
It would take more than just a dream
To sail beyond the things I've seen
More than the woman who finally appeared
Too late for me to care
Beyond the currency of appease
I use to blanket me.
I came to a place
Where I could live without a name
Needed to be a shadow so I could see
And the whispers upon their breaths
would be mine alone
This is what happens when you have no home.
But maybe when I wake It'll be alright...

-Surroundings-

Clutter.
The mind cluttered
My shelves cluttered
My boxes
Neat
Yet
Cluttered
With comforts I've placed upon myself
Overwhelmingly
Cluttered
With those possible things
Physical
Social
Mental
Which I begged to need
Just to avoid the knowledge
I really didn't
Need or want the clutter of true
Existence.
It is my new winter
My changing year
A chance to disrobe my inequities...
I wonder if I can find an amazing sale?

-Cosmos-

Across the divide I stare
Searching for your flicker of recognition
Wondering just how long ago
The radiance of your love
Was cast to me.

-Nearly There-

They all were so close
Nearly there
Perfection just an issue away
But I couldn't stay within the lines.
I have a habit of coloring beyond borders;
Taking my strokes too seriously
I attempt to make it all so seamless
Photogenic
Until that smear
The blemish which begs redo
Ultimately knowing I will not be satisfied
And so
Crumple that canvas once so promising
It was just a copy anyway...

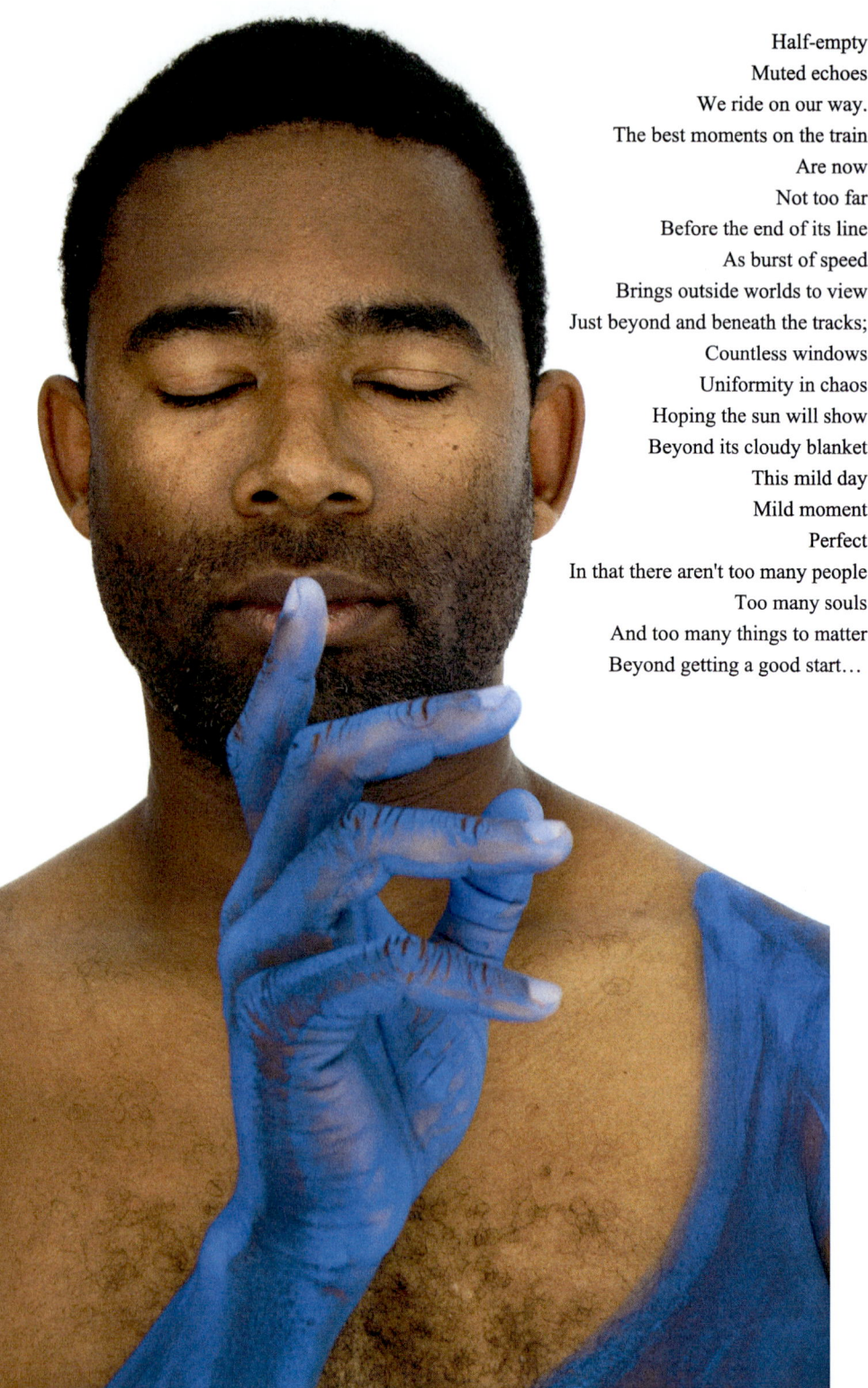

-Uno Momento-

Half-empty
Muted echoes
We ride on our way.
The best moments on the train
Are now
Not too far
Before the end of its line
As burst of speed
Brings outside worlds to view
Just beyond and beneath the tracks;
Countless windows
Uniformity in chaos
Hoping the sun will show
Beyond its cloudy blanket
This mild day
Mild moment
Perfect
In that there aren't too many people
Too many souls
And too many things to matter
Beyond getting a good start…

-Alabaster Smile-

Reading and searching for something interesting
Alabaster smile sits across
Nods
Goes Jolly Rancher interpretation
Enticing
Bringing me to recognize
The way eyes look upward and away
Sucking slowly upon fructose simplicity
Drawing attention to deep cocoa skin
Velvet smooth
As swimming becomes daydream
Bittersweet upon my tongue
Rolled upon my palate
Leaving me wanting
Despite my taken position.
Alabaster smile
Hands folded, locking
Protecting emotions I selfishly think similar;
And I'm wanting honeyed juice
Midnight hopes upon my twilight truths…
What was that saying?
The darker the berry,
The sweeter the proof?

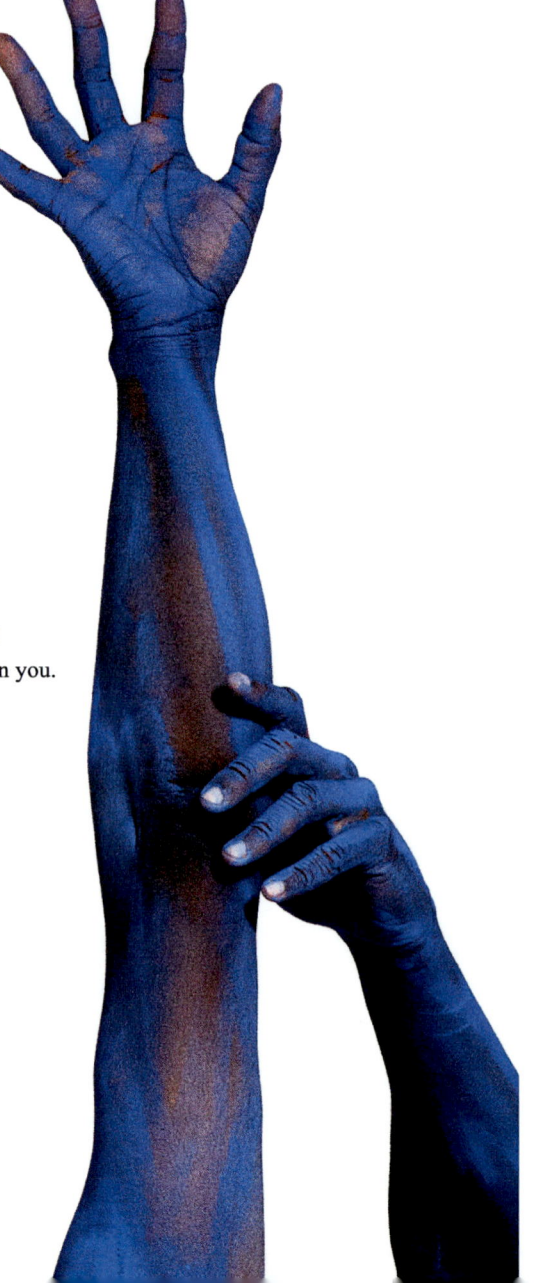

-Delayed-

You are beautiful.
Point blank
A creation complex
I want to visit again
And again
In this museum of ages.
You peer down
To the side
Any way to avoid me;
Knowing I stare across this void
This place in shambles
As others look to me
Thinking
They
Are the inspiration for my eyes
Upon and beyond.
I watch your spread
Think how I'd love your spread
Despite;
In spite of those things which haunt my mind
When it comes to the perfection I witnessed in you.
I think you question.
I think you curious of natures
And these railways beneath...
You want express to thine heart,
But there is only local
Left behind
Forced to clean up the mess
Of another possible love
Exiting too many stops too soon.

-Shuffle-

Shifts methodical,
I stare into tomorrow's poker face
Waiting for my wilds,
My virtually anythings
To fill these gaps
About this hand dealt to me.
My cohorts jovial displays
Seek to remind
I'm always dealing
With the bottom of a deck
I'd swear was stacked with each new hand
Each evolving challenge
Every sinister display
As everyday evolves into faces
Numbers
And sweets too rich
I am stricken with a severe case
Of the runaways
From this and that
And the constant moves
To trip me
Force me
Con me
Into revealing every single minuscule thing
I could possibly be
Come into this age of endless chance...

-Around The Lake-

I ran beneath stars this early
morning
Ran beneath the dawning of love's
embrace
As she lifted her eyelids
Pointed her sapphire gaze upon
me
Welcoming mine own
As I became lost within the sheer
breeze
Of her gown upon my face with
each
new step.
I thought to myself
'Why are you so far?'
Heard my lungs exhale my desire
To race to thee over and over
again
To be lost in the shadows of the
morning
Which exist only fleetingly
Because fate
The inevitable color which drowns
Comes all too fast to blur mine
vision
Until I am able to sleep at last
In the midnight of your embrace.

-The First Morning-

Perfection moves forward
One stop at a time
In the rare silence of this morning
Which won't last
As every morning to follow
There will be more
And I will have to juggle
Between my thoughts
And their unknown stories.
Now I see uniformity
Along with someone's attempt
To brighten this place
This void of light
Tucked impeccably beneath
the chaos above;
I hear echoes
Of countless souls who've passed
Along this very line;
See their faces
In these sporadic lights passing
Imprinting
their movement upon these pages
To ultimately hope
I will not just be another shadow
Another echo
Waiting to be caught
Upon a glimpse
As these moments move further
Along time's route.

-TT-

Right
now I'm missing it
Thinking on it again too much
To a point I know
Where if I close my eyes
I'd wake up there
And I wouldn't want to return.
You see, right now
I'm wanting it
Thinking of every way possible to get it
To a point of necessity
Damn near a tragedy
Because I know It's of no use to me
At least upon the facade these streets see
As I'm shuffling
Caught in one too many lines
While trying to get back to me
Without seeming selfish and needy.
But if I wake up there,
I'm afraid I'll never leave...

-The Blame Game-

Can't blame you
For winds howling beyond my door
For rains seeping through these panes
Loose from neglect
Parched and cracked
Like the fibers of my heart.
Can't blame you
But would love to
Because it would be better
Than sitting here
Abusing myself
Trying to make apologies
For things I'll never understand.
Can't blame you
But want to
Paint you red with my sorrow
Then black with my existence
Only to erase you with my truth
I am somewhere between
Asset and liability
When it comes to love.
Can't blame you
But I'll think about it
Cry
Only to think about it some more…

-Damaged Goods-

The damage done
All I can do now
Is be
Hoping I'll catch notice of the
wind
To alter myself
Just enough to avoid total
destruction.
Unbalanced material
Symmetry broken
I, dying leaf
Colors drained
Wait to crumble beneath,
Upon these paths of the living;
Damage done
All I can do now
Is waste away;
A collection of unfinished
thoughts
Of tears dripping only now
From my pen
Because I am depleted of emotion
Left with words which exist
Only to hurt,
Turn away
Leaving me sorry for my
existence.
The damage is done
So why bother?

-Unconscious Alteration-

Wheeling these streets
Faded hues speak.
Everywhere I look
Snapshots spring forward of what used to be
As I hear our younger selves call.
Stories froth within my mind
Leaving me with just as many questions
As I had before I had so many answers;
Where did we go wrong?
Was this God's punishment
That our laborers would be damned
Haunted by our stumblings careless
Intentional with the weight of excuse
That this is a hard world...
The neurosis of my instant self
Against these parched and peeling images
Somehow intently tucked away in my parents closets
Bonded to a degree that to separate them
Would mean a loss of history
Verification
That those captured souls had even existed,
Overtakes me
Rears it's appetite to destroy me
With each new loss
To the former glory
I only now realize we'd existed in...
Wheeling these streets
My routes to expiation explained
I again shift the stitching of my seams.

-Highland Shadow-

Faith,
That powerful motivator
Descends each time I grace these
walls
Walk these paths of mine history.
I lose myself
Wonder
Does my deity,
or the faith of these old souls
protect me?
Do prayers travel upon the breeze
Following the coast of my
existence
To settle upon me
Wrap themselves around my
branches
Through my leaves
To cause me to sing this song
Survival
And it's delicate variations
For my forest to hear?
For Jesus is real?
For real?
For living is real
Death is mystery
Faith, obedience
Obedience, structure
An attachment to that which
Methodically
Is torn down by it's very architect
Truth.
Each time I return
I understand a little more
Acquiescence a little more
Because the spirit too is me
Despite my will to abolish it
From those fields of my follies...

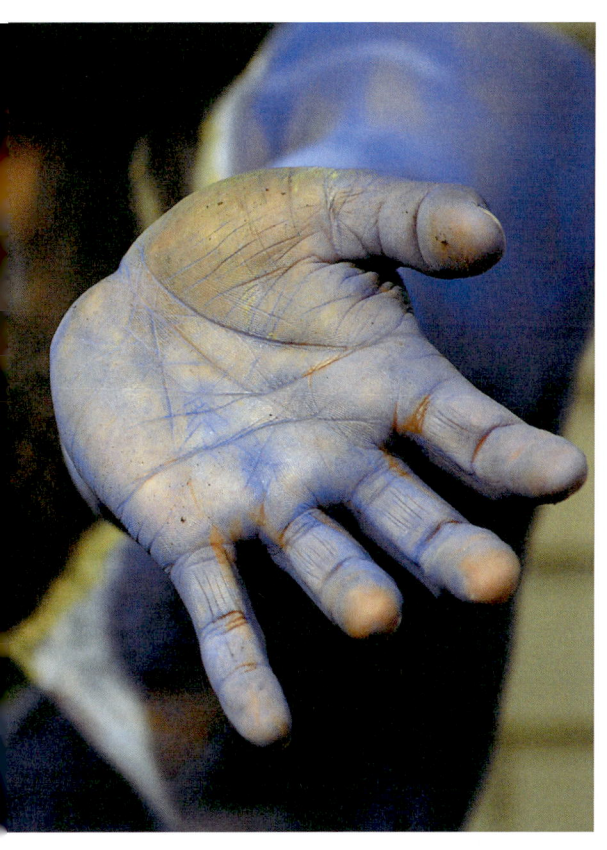

-Honor-

Honoring your name
The spirit begs me to move;
Why am I so still?

-Caramel-

He peeped her
Stared her down
Undressed her caramel
And let slip his mind's tongue
Over her delicacies.
She saw him
Dismissed him
Figuring her coffee had enough cream
And a desperate nature
From even a god
Is best to avoid;
She saw him
Dismissed the thing
Which others more subtle
Wrapped within dreams
Because a candy this sweet
Was placed too high on the shelf
Behind glass
With a price tag
As rich as her caramel fantasy.
He peeped her
Dipped into his mind's pockets
Only to find change
Peeped her some more
Daydreaming the moment
When he could unwrap her
Place her upon his palate
Letting the heat of his desire melt her
As her caramel essence
Brought a smile to his face.

-Mind Lay-

He saw me
Peeped me
Knew me
Deep into the stranger
Mystery.
Did he feel it?
Thoughts upon stranger tides;
Could he feel it?
Kisses,
Sighs,
Saying goodbyes?
This tearful game of madness
Shouts
Suburbia dreams
Antiquated ideas
Da da-daaah
Duh duh-da
And words don't equate clear
So I ponder
His depths of me
Iris deep
Contemplating
Why
I'm looking upon
One too many
Searching for the faint inspiration
Of adultery...

-In Passing-

Nature paints a glimpse.
The greater picture hidden
Found only with time.

-Let That Be A Lesson-

It was silent as I looked up and saw him.

Unusual

Because his is the mouth which never ceases.

I waited, but beyond his greeting

Silence.

Morning.

Early.

We engrossed ourselves in caffeine

Print, and whatever else would ease us into reality.

Silence.

I relished this moment

Knowing it wouldn't last;

His conspirators waited

Along with his vernacular spout never slowing.

I hoped the example of us 'working folk'

Would saturate his being

Permeate what things he would choose to learn

Today

Tomorrow

And far beyond those stale paths

Some would desire for him.

My future...

Go figure.

-WATER-

'Good words cool more than cold water'

-John Ray-

-Azul-

Sand passed through age's glass
Each grain an echo to the one before;
They used to be shouts
Now demure and subdued
They are whispers
Quiet private memories
And smiles at how those were the times.
Blue enveloped the soul
As it had before and would again
Despite heart's smoldering furnace
Ever yearning for release
Cataclysmic recognition
In the jealousy it had to share the vessel;
And you,
You rose like the sun
Bringing warmth
Breathing life into the night which became of the blue.
You followed
Remaining constant
And peace took that azure being
Ignited it's heart
Made heavy it's thoughts on your demise
Retreat,
Back to a place of cold longing
And too many stars against the blanket of night that blue did slip beneath.
Blue counted the sands
Echoing as they fell
Until eyes trembled to life
To find you in sight
Dreams come true eventually
Just as kisses become breath
Eventually one
Blue
Infinite.

-Idea-

Rue the core of men
Deceptively full of light
Beliefs petrified.

-It-

I can't stop thinking
The effect has me full
Yet wanting still to cup my hands beneath the stream
Of sober intoxication
Inebriated wisdom
That clarity which arrives
On steeds wild
Trampling the plains of my mind
As they race ahead of reality's front,
Ominously approaching.

-The Great Divide-

Put two pennies together
Called it a date
Two dimes
Called it escape
Two nickels
Only to discover life
Was an unfathomable pickle
Of one bill upon another;
I asked for it
Prayed for it
Laid for it
Forgetting myself
Put two together
Only to discover
It wasn't enough
And was never going to be.
Put two quarters together
Called it a meal
Spent two dollars
Thought it was a steal
And thus I am still
Bound by the ramifications
Of a people and a place
That hadn't the time
To educate about these things
These pairings of persistence
Marauders
Murderers of the soul
Which cause one to dream;
Work for it
Steal for it
Lie for it
And you know the rest...

-A Matter of Time-

How I wish that you were mine
Time.
How I long to have you
Steal you away from your love
Fate.
How I dream you;
Envision you laying your secrets
Only to mine ears.
To dance with you
Partner you
Waltz you until we are one
And eternity is our playground
In life
Never in death's black slumber.
How I wish that you were mine...

-Good Morning Baltimore-

Good morning Baltimore
I'm sorry to hear
that your people are living in fear
Your streets are on fire and the reason
is clear
But sad to say it's just the atmosphere
Innocence died a long time ago
Unfortunately ignorance is still here
Ferguson to Oklahoma to the Carolinas
Within the un-united states
it's an ongoing drama
Perpetual
Institutional mistakes on both sides
Stories now muddled across digital lies
Darken a hope I once witnessed in eyes
Leaving hollow shells for the world to
despise.
I said
Good morning Baltimore
it's time for the weather
I wish my tears could put out your fires
forever
But the depths of this chasm
Known as racial divide
Reach to that core
Where our molten will lies
And so it ends with ash in the air
Ends with another city
full of pain and despair

And this I wish
That our nation was fair
But it pains me to say
It's just the atmosphere...
Good morning Baltimore
Let's have a moment of prayer
Think about our children
And the world we prepare
Never forget the fires we ignite
They will inherit in an ongoing fight
For a chance to breathe
For a chance to be seen

Beyond the amber of their skin
As human beings;
'But what again!?'
I hear you scream in frustration
'Will come from the lies
used to divert this nation?'
'And how again,
can we attempt to do right,
if acknowledgment only comes
when we turn and we fight?'
(Yeah) good morning Baltimore
Know that we feel your pain
From the west to the east
North to south it's the same
And I wish that I could say
tomorrow's forecast is better
But feeling the winds,
I'm only sensing disaster
As again we cry
Again we drown in our tears
Bend but never break within this
atmosphere.

-Watchstop-

60
Seconds to pray the DJ won't stop
This groove
Washing over me
Causing me to feel
50
Feet high
Despite my lack of mule and
40
Acres to grow
Plant
Entrench
My seed
The longevity of me
Upon this swirl amongst swirls.
Now beyond
30
I look at decisions
Reverse how I got here
Ask
Seriously?
Was it that easy to change course?
Of course,
Hindsight
20/20
I find my balance lies in
understanding
I can and shall
Just as this rhythm flows
With ease and purpose
To move all whom hear to that end
Some

10
Steps in the making
Beyond
9
Moments of regret,
8
Minutes of pleasure
And the
7
Sins they encompassed
As
6
Wishes turned memories
Found me
5
Fingers away
From that ultimate touch
As I reached
4
Heaven,
That divine
3
Father
Son
Holiness
2
Make myself complete
In that
1
Selection...

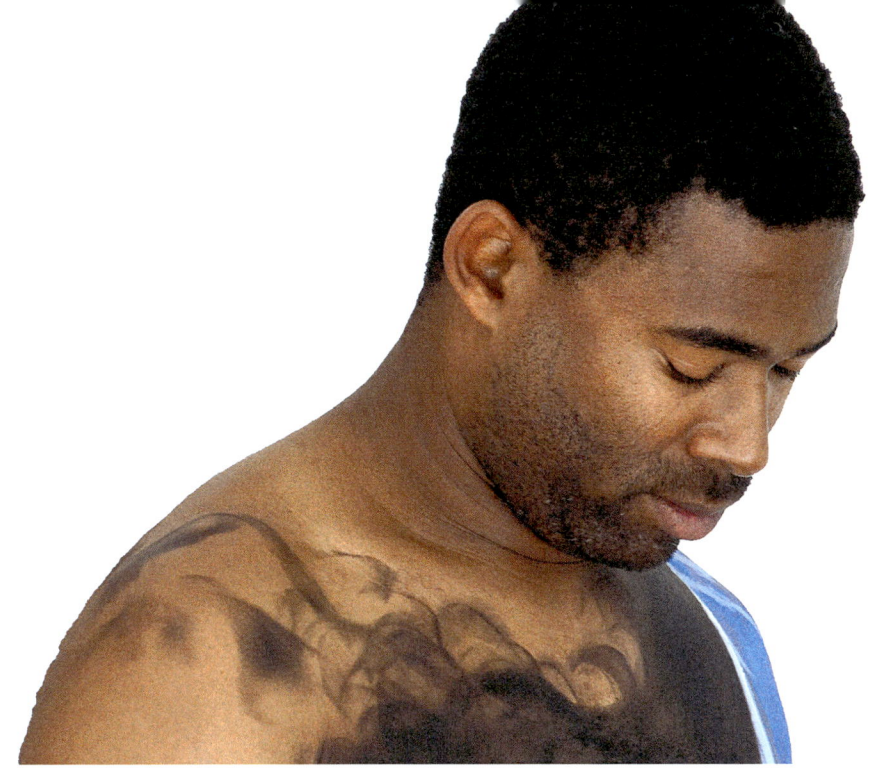

-Butterscotch Cocoa-

Butterscotch cocoa
Makes me wanna go-go
Dream
Underneath the flowers
Lazily beside the stream.
Butterscotch cocoa
How you gonna go-go
Smiling at me
Then never want to follow
When I wanna go-go
Down your stream?
Butterscotch cocoa
Why is love a no-no
And while we're at it
Why you staring at me?
You make me wanna go-go
Somewhere that's a no-no
To play with flowers in my dreams.

Maybe you don't know so
Despite the fact I say so;
Maybe you don't care so
Maybe I should go-go

Butterscotch cocoa
You're the only one I want to taste
Despite the overflow so
Of all the other sweets in this place;
And would it be a low blow
To say I think it quite so
That you get a kick out of watching
me crave?
I think I need to go-go
If it's only just a no-no
The contents behind your wrapper
embrace.

-Internal Affair-

Sometimes
I think I couldn't love you more.
Like trying to find another reason to love
Love
It breaches upon impossible
In a repetitive world of clichés
Forget-me-nots
Not out of genuine emotion
Rather that unconscious knowledge
That unless we do things otherwise
It's just a matter of time before we dissipate
Beyond memory
Into the sheer nothingness of passing.
Sometimes I stumble on you
A path I thought familiar
Memorized down to those basic details
Even I forget to notice in myself;
Stumble because you surprise me
In the answers to those questions of you
Leaving me lost in my heart's labyrinth
Hoping not to run into the beast of survival
I created to guard those fragile chambers.
Sometimes I create you
Momentarily forgetting who you are
And need
You to do the same;
Wash me anew
Equating me to those fantasies which drive you,
Will you
When something about me
Just won't do.
I couldn't love you more
Than I have
Do now
Will in perpetuity
As the residuals of fate's episodes
Rain upon me
Leaving me to drown in you.

-Forget Me Not-

He made me forget
Mistakes
Made me toss rationale aside
Till all there was left
Was gut
Raw
Uninhibited emotion
And new beginnings
Volatile and exquisite,
Like new worlds forming.
With him I wanted to see
Photographs and memories
On night stands and book shelves
Covered in age's dust
And people smiling because
Well,
Just because it was us
As if it always was
And only time was the culprit
Keeping us apart.
He made me touch desire;
Made it a tangible thing
I could somehow wrap myself within
During those cold callous moments
Chalked up to life
So I could be at peace
Dreaming time was the only culprit
And not my unfortunate realities
In keeping us apart.
He made me forget
Me
Remembering only the ambrosia of his smile
Sweetness honey-suckle kisses
Stolen between leaves
As they turned a deeper shade of love
Only to fall dead and dying
In that fall of confusion
To yet be reborn
When at last we could be in presence.

-Thus-

He spoke the truth
And it struck my ears with joy.
A chance
Real chance
Water on thirst's horizon
I longed more than ever then
In that pure revelation
To drink him
Quench my aching need
Rejuvenate
Returning to my summer self
during my current winter of discontent;
Disconnect.
I stared upon memories
Moving further into a past
I long to make current,
And smiled
Thinking 'one day'
Kisses won't be so far
And those emotions will remain present-tense
In those verses I sing
Think on
Dream on
When it comes to this mate
My soul has chosen...
And thus all would be well and warm
Instead of fleeting
As my exhales against this cold which only greets me now.

-Face To Face-

I came upon truth at the summit
Approached cautiously, because it has a way
Of hurting
Inflicting a pain one can never know if they are ready for
Or not.
There within the violet and saffron hues of a setting sun
Our palaver commenced;
I accepted some revelations with ease
While others caused anger to swell,
It is never easy to see one's reflection for the first time.
Truth laughed heartily, Paused a moment,
Then withdrew a cigarette and lit it in the most deliberate fashion.
it was the swell before the surge;
A destructive wave
Cast about from my tsunami of existence
Sent to wash over me, Drown me
Erode the very foundation of me
Till I was nothing but grains of moments
Hoping to coalesce on the shores of memory;
Someone's.
Anyone's.
Truth paused, Inhaled
Held that thought and watched me
Waited on me to break
Then exhaled through a set of gritted teeth.
Was it frustration?
I could not decipher through the ribbons of smoke now caressing it's orifice.
Speaking,
That single word speared me,
Harpooned my core and bled me of everything I thought I knew;
Thought I wanted to know.
And reaching for the nearest projectile
I realized there was nothing to grab but my own consciousness
Now hollow and weightless.
Try as I may
That single word escapes me
Teases me in shadow
Just as truth meant it I'm sure,
Has me searching the libraries of my world awake
Longing.

-38-

Sunlight whispers secrets to my dreams
Wakes me reminiscing of things
I can't begin to explain;
The desert of my conscience waits for a rain.
Flower's petals bloom to reveal universe's essence and still
I long for God to explain
Why with this forest in bloom is there so much rain?
Huddled in the darkness of my mind
I embark on a journey to find
Answers to my pain
Explanations for my rains flooding the fields of me;
My attempts to swim so vain.
Sunlight peeks through the window at me
Fading from clouds upon the horizon I see
Again, I can't begin to explain
That beckoning chorus
Just ahead of those rains.
One would think I've learned by now
To shelter and save
Keep my soul from drowning
Within the storm's wake
One would think I'd be satisfied
Head above the waves
Moving ever-forward towards that land upon the horizon,
But no, it escapes me,
Because there are always adventures in the wait
New and stunning, they creep through my murk to find me
Again, each and every time though I try escape
Because pain is comfort
And that window for change seems to only come
This time of the year along this side of a beer
And yes, the explicit tear
Protruding but never quite falling
From this side of me
As the sun sets and I make blessings of regrets...

-Courtney-

You kissed me divine.
Tasted like lavender.
Stood against the russet brick aglow
From the only warmth the sun would provide
And chuckled in a way I was too naive to know
I was the subject of conversation.
But now I know.
You kissed me divine.
Wanted me out of mystery I assume.
Or was it a challenge?
Spun me with your eyes
Knew me all too well;
Yes, you knew us all too well.
I know this now too.
You kissed me divine.
Your scent was of lavender;
I walked home that day elated
With every other step
Afraid with every other;
One fell swoop I knew I was not a man
Just a boy with nothing
Your gift a precious thing of memory
Before even the scent could dissipate.
You kissed me divine.
And I thought of your lavender
One day which stretched on for years
Gave rise to my insatiable passions
Till there was no boy, but man
Understanding that his very core could not exist without your history;
Without those precious gifts you bestowed
For whatever reason...
Curiosity?
As I now know, well,
That's just for me.

-Half Me-

I see him and wish he were mine.
Wish my influence wasn't so bound
To the minute and second hands of our environ.
Everyday he smiles, and though fleetingly,
I find that I'm staring at myself
A carbon copy from another universe;
I try my best to warn him
Accolade him when apropos
Joke with him that I couldn't be his dad
When in truth, I could so be.
He is the culmination of my fears and possibilities
Slipping further away to that unknown place
Not quite regret;
He is the hand I've longed to take
Since I was a boy
'Three sons' I'd said, before I realized
Responsibility and reproduction often now
Need to go hand-in-hand;
His is the face I see when she walks by
And I visually splice an offspring.
Maybe that's why it also sickens me to see him,
This dream,
Behind my eyelids so long, I know it when I'm awake,
Because as long as I'm here,
Others will come
And I can only hope this feeling
As with all things reconciled
Will pass away
Each time the mirror of ages reminds
That it all ends with me
And nothing will go on...

-Early-Morning Train-

A rumble in the distance tells me I'm here
The tumble of my stomach warns me of fear
Somewhere out beyond my windows it creeps
And I should be crying.
Someone doesn't want me angry today
I don't want to see myself go that way
Somewhere in the dark it's creeping
I'm up and yet I know I should be sleeping;
But that's what has me up here in the morn
Sleeping with these enemies that I scorn
At every turn I feel they're trying to kill me
Nullify me like my government completely
As somewhere beyond these windows it creeps
Resolutions set to pull me in deep
Beyond a truth that I know the train is lying
And with each swipe I know I should be crying...

-Possibly, Definitely-

On a line
Possibly definitely
I give in
To this vision of things
I think could lift me
Bring chocolates and roses
To the place in my dreams
Where admiring melds into loving
Heavy petting
Possibly, definitely a little seat wetting;
But back to my waiting.
On a line
Possibly, definitely
Coming up with excuses for my
daydreamings
Wanderings
And too many hidden paths enticing
Providing that release I find lacking
In my possibly, definitely
I envision every time the skies are grey
And I am shuttered underneath
My prerequisite blacks
Longing for my pastel springs
Clashing summers
And just plain exploring;
But back to my standing
In a line
As crowds are rotating
Eyes avoiding this tasteless scene
A man alone unmoving
Despite their quiet pleading for skedaddle
A returning to the end of the line
Assuming possibly, definitely
It is the only place I've known
Broken of desire
To let loose the tit of survival
Now withered and raw
Producing only dust
To settle upon my collections of possibly...

Definitely.

-Shower Scene-

Tonight I scrubbed you away.
Took the pumice to my soul;
Deeper the back and forth until it became caked
With the flakes of your promises
Once healthy and new
Now just a residue I watch a steady stream
Pound and flush away.
Tonight I watched you go.
Quietly you fled just as you'd entered my life
Settled upon me
Stained me
Made me stink of you
Till I was unrecognizable
And all there was left of me
Was a somber core
Wrought with failing and crime.
Tonight,
I felt you flee.
You knew there was no more
Us;
That I could no longer support your fantasy
And you could neither fulfill my persistent needs
Too false and burdened of hope over action.
We parted,
And devoid of you
I was left to know
Whom I truly was and capable of being...

Thank you.

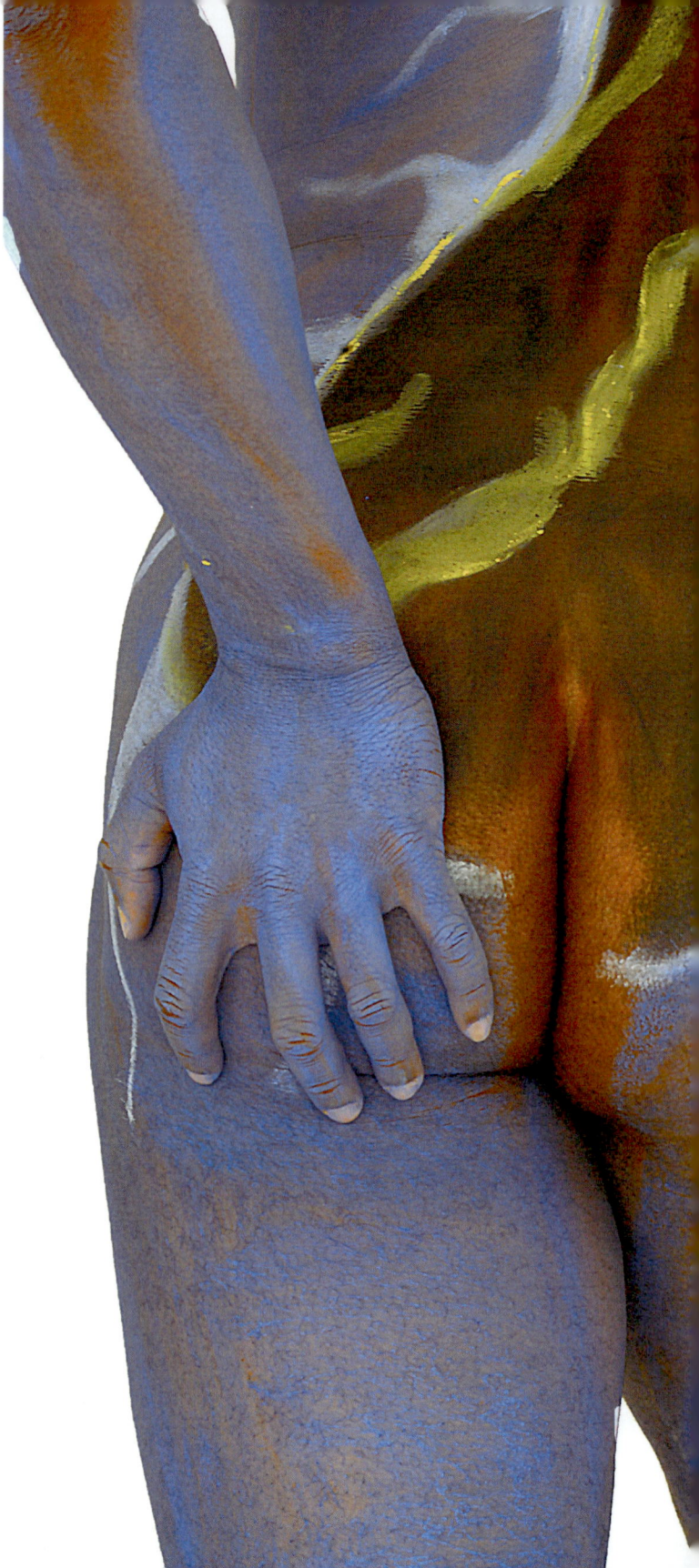

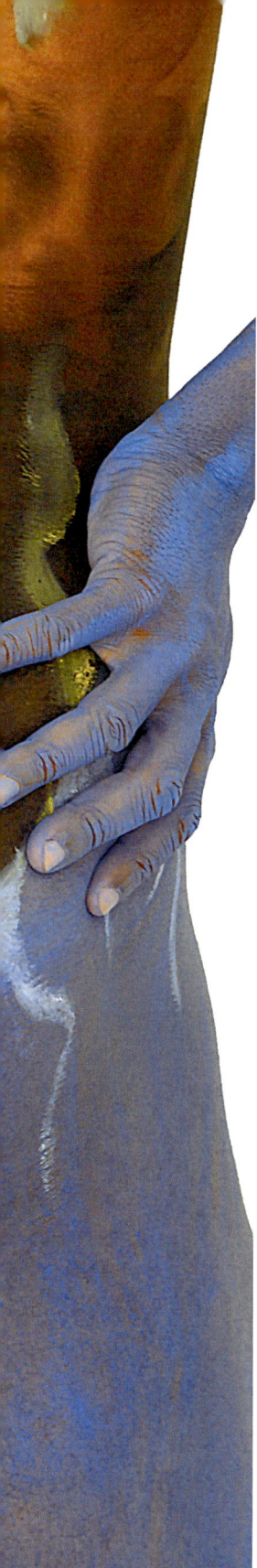

-The Hunt-

Right now in this early hour
In the moisture of this morning's growing dew
I want to hunt.
I want to close my eyes and listen for you
Hear those creatures of the night as they seek me too;
I want my heart to race with fear and excitement
My prize
A capture or two
Maybe you;
I want euphoria sustained
For my flesh to tingle
Mingle with the brush
As deliberate footfalls and hushed conversations
Between the creatures of the night
Make for bedtime stories
Tomorrow with drinks and friends;
My prize
A capture or two
Maybe you
Right now in this early hour
In the slow of the sun's rise
Just beyond the point of too late to care,
I want to hunt.
I want to open my soul to the trees
And creatures watching amongst them
As I reconnect to my self
That part of me I cannot explain
Don't want to explain
Just enjoy
Primal
Needing and wanting
Having to conquer
Despite my belly full
A prize
Maybe two...
Maybe you.

-Prayer Beyond Sunset-

Blue moon sings sweet and low
A delicate tune to open my eyes
Turn the air that surrounds
To something which slows
My thoughts
Allowing me to see clearly
Despite these tainted goggles which grace my face.
Blue moon as I cross the ever again
And promises spoken in haste return;
Children angry anointed with the failings of their father.
Save me...
Blue moon answers back to me
That I already know the answers
To the riddles I produce.
Blue me

Blue moon upon my tongue as stars fall
As unanswered conundrums,
Twisted tones as blues turn to blacks
And midnight's back to me
Scarred and desperate for minutes more to rule
Before sunrise has it's fun...
Blue moon speaks to blue me
Blue eyes which see
And shed blue tears
Because there are no other shades
No other fates
And truth will cease to reveal itself.
Amen.

-Ocean Ave. Blue Note-

Navy blue collar gave way
To baby blue collar high rise;
Joe the bum,
always earning with a joke,
Got killed in a stroller drive-by;
My grease spot's now gluten-free
And there's no pork to go on my rye
I'd tell 'em all to go to hell
If I thought it'd make it right.
If I thought it'd make it right,
I'd scream from my lungs,
Paint the streets with my rage
Dark crimson mentality
Flowing
Trickle to stream
To flooding history
Life;
And therein lies the problem
This metamorphosis is life
Constant as the minutes before
And those which are to be born
Of that exact need to survive
surrounding all we know to exist.
The feeding
Gorging, purging;
Digestion
is the synopsis of this
and other places;
Here it just goes a little faster.
The metropolitan vessel churns
Lubricated by the change it's masses bring
Hurling themselves upon it's gears
In an attempt to belong to the current pace of things
Which tomorrow,
shall be relegated only to memory.

-Solitary Stool Sampling-

Everyone's away.
For a moment, soon,
For a lifetime
Extended drive
Flight
Train
Dare I say, bus ride
Away.

In this passing moment
I hear their voices
My response to their lament
That love and company are non-existent
Away from them, though fleetingly close
Like those moments of death ever-present
We don't think about because, well
They're away
Rapping upon someone else's door
A raven to that whatever was lost

This side of age

Off-center to wisdom and
chances taken no longer
Due to chills and apparitions
of dead presidents
Taking flights of stupidity
because well,
One should know better...

by now.

I miss them all.
Miss them,
selfishly wish them here
Instead of this libation of
loneliness.

Shit,
I'm headed for trouble...

I'm at a loss
Crossroads maybe?
I want to dine alone, but here in
solitude amongst the crowd
And I am coward
Longing for even hollow
laughter
Cordial acknowledgment
So it doesn't feel so far
Despite my ear next to this
thumping speaker of joy.

Away.
And I wish what was mine,
shared more in conjunction with me;
Crystal vs opaque
Instant vs painstaking time
Subtlety
A scream over silence to be heard
Away
As knowledge cascades...

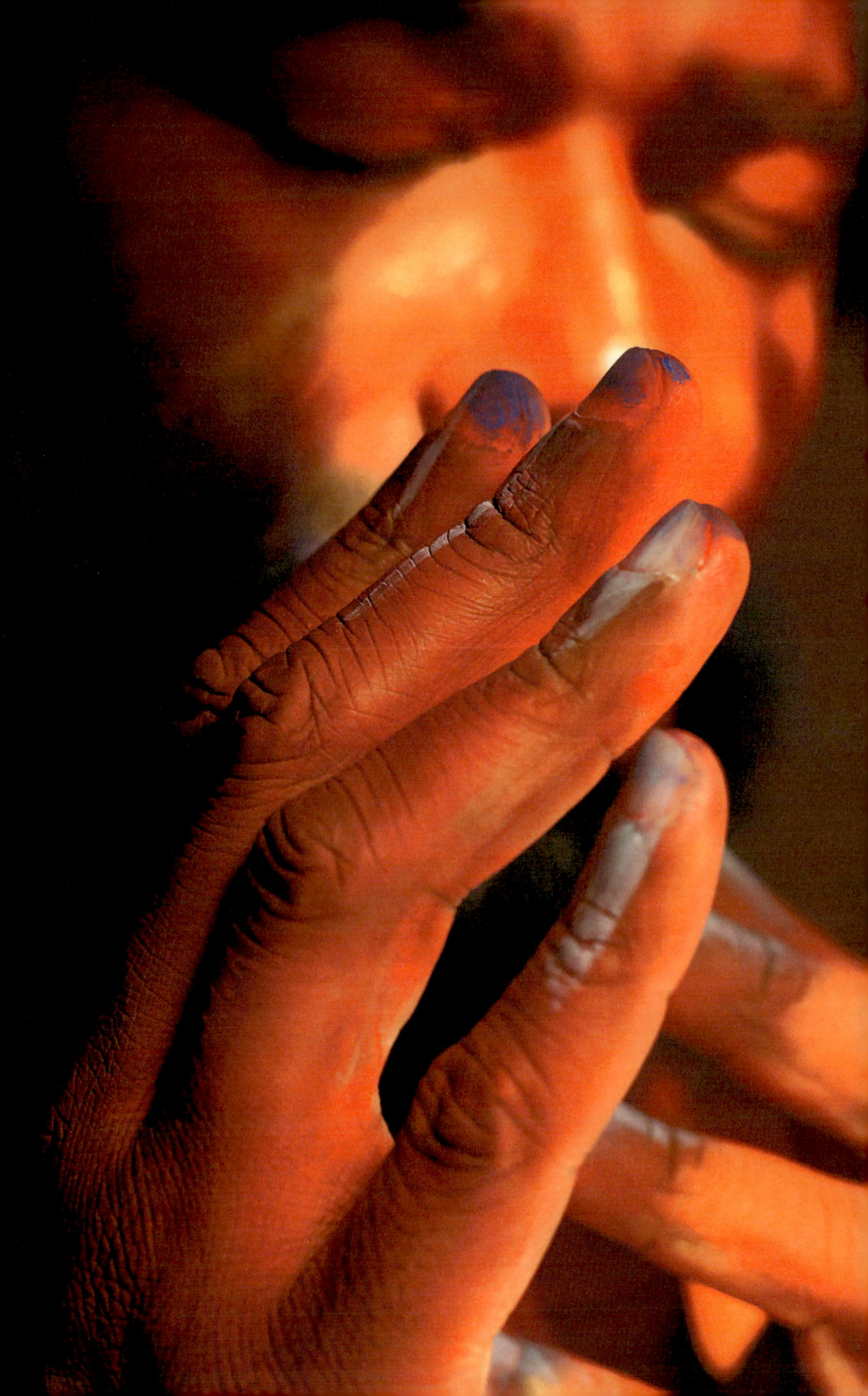

-FIRE-

'I threw myself into that fire, threw myself into it...
and let myself burn'
-Sarah J. Maas-

-Done-

Said it best
'Spare the rod, spoil the child.'
Yes, I recognize that I live in a different world
Recognize that I am a relic
Another antiquated piece of history
My nation works at erasing
Eradicating from it's pages
Until sheets are left riddled with stains
From words and deeds now apparitions
And bullet holes where our collective soul drained
To again fuel
As it did before
Our captors greed.
Yes, I got whipped as a child
Whooped as a child
Beat
As a child;
To that end, I am now loathed
Because I say 'yes 'mam'
'No sir' and think to nod in acknowledgment
Of another human being
Another struggle
Another sense of purpose
And, hell
Just to brighten someone's day.
I got a beat-down every so often
For my actions
And the fact I repeatedly tried to have things go
My way;
Crossed boundaries
And refused to
Get with the program
Of survival out of love
And ensuring I was a productive citizen
Able to hold my own
Know my worth
And never let a system make decisions for me
That I should be making for myself.

I got tore up
Marked up even once
My mother so tired of my lies and attempts
To publicly humiliate her that she
Needed to go there
Needed to get in that ass to such a degree...
Parenting it was called
Better to sting for a little now
Than to hurt for a lifetime
Fuel for a lifetime
My country's need
To keep a nigger in place
Because the heart of the place
Puritanical
Only recycles the same blood it shed to exist;
Because the soul of this place...
Well, does an animal even have one?
So to answer the question on your mind,
Yes, I would strike my child
Whip my flesh
Spank my blood
Get into that ass
And love them
Love them
Pray them understanding
Hope them strong respectful minds
That understand the nature of the beast
Which lies in wait behind these Stars and
Stripes
Ready to devour
Masticate them spiritually
Masturbate them commercially
And shit them out
Into the next ghetto province it seeks to
create...

-39-

If ignition is conception
That first spark then tendril of life,
I am fire
Melodious and destructive
I breathe fascination
Outlined
In fear
Though with knowledge,
Respect
As my depictions
Of love, war, and survival
Singe the flesh of those who'd dance with me
Lost
Entranced in their attempt to mold
That which shapes
And shifts
Returning everything to it's origin
Dust
To cake the lungs of the living
Now unto forever.

-Sonny-

Time's contradiction
Edges upon my borders;
Youth's price fully paid.

-Six Fifteen Fourteen-

You want words
Want love, I don't know I can give
Caught upon a past paradise
Without sin you live
Leaving me these days
To try
Coming up with some reason to praise
The way they do
When it comes to you, untouchable
But I can only drown in the proof...
Afterthought
I languish behind
You summed it up when you said
'I prefer' another kind
Please keep your hurt
On a day like this
I've enough to go around the sun,
A light I could never be
Still I long for words of honesty
To show a mortal side
A human face
God afforded you
The chance to misplace;
You want words?
Or maybe it's my heart?
My submission?
For me to go in your way?

I know, 'God's'
It comes back to a light
A mystery
A dying uniformity
just to get you by
Just to give you hope,
Something I clung to every night,
That somehow I'd awake
and I'd make it right;
This day,
I'm pained to say,
I wish would just go away.
You want what she gives
Despite the sins
She lingers
Depends
Fulfills your fantasy,
I now,
Only have words
To taste my anger
To make up for your hurt
And questions
I have no strength to ask
For all that it's worth
To hear three words
Even now I'm unsure I could utter
Meaningfully
When it comes down to us.
Three words which haunt vividly
Still
Because it continues
This regurgitation of your...
(exhale)
I wish I could tire,
Of hating you both.

-Basin-

I wanted to write a letter,
But that seemed too formal for our affair.
Wanted to look back and find the semblance
Reasons and acknowledgments of those things which freshly haunt
Of the light seeker
And the fact that you, unlike anyone else,
Enabled because, as you stated,
You always had a preference for females
(Thanks for the confirmation of me being an afterthought)....
I wanted to write you a letter while breath still caressed your lungs
Not for closure, but to witness any thought of hope fade
In our understanding each other;
This monster you created in me, has no more tears to shed
Has no more heart to break
Devoid of all longing
It has nothing left, other than to feed upon itself
A continuous self-sustaining act
Which allows me to exist somewhere on the borders of heaven and hell;
Purgatory maybe?
That just makes me come off as adolescent
But my gaping wound will not close to heal.
Even if you did right by me from beyond the grave
I have enough years to haunt me
Reminding no amount of breath
No amount of characters scribed or verses memorized from your god to mine
Could polish the shit you perpetrated so willingly.
Once you assumed I would take your offer
That I was afraid of the world you were ready to cast me out into
Unprepared
(Purposefully perhaps?)
But I left anyways
Stumbled over and over again
Until I was myself
A man
Sitting here now trying his best to thank a person
Who never once genuinely seemed thankful for him,
A consolation
Pacification of sorts

Still waiting...

-That Time Again-

So here I am
In thought again
Beneath cumulus decisions
As I make my way past fields
Overgrown
with desperation
And a content destructive, stunning.
Somewhere amongst these paths
I exist
Wonder whether dreams
As mine
Are seductively
Unconsciously peppered with regret
And a longing for completion
A full circle of strength,
And a balance,
Which in my age I've come to learn
Come only with dialogue.
First external.
A sharing of knowledge
In preparation of futures uncertain
With that persistent factor
Time
And a fact it only favors those whom prepare
Run head-first into it
Knowing they cannot conquer,
But can become palatable manipulators.

External

Behind closed doors

Full of history

An understanding of foundations placed

Before

And before that

Yet still before them

And the steady destruction brought

By others who've mastered the manipulation

Of the collective mind.

External

As in language and dialogue

Presentation

And the fact you cannot change your skin

However you can your tone

And actions which communicate a thirst

For knowledge

Beyond sidewalks and trappings

Masqueraded as freedoms

As choice.

External;

I remember when he said

'understand and always be aware of your surroundings'

For once you truly see where you are

You will certainly understand where it is you want to go

And how to get there

Avoiding the obstacles bound to be placed in your path

Leading to dialogs

Internal

And desires to never perpetrate those things

They

Would have

Us

To be...

-Recede-

Not enough time between stations anymore
Never enough time on platforms
To extrapolate and thus form
Staccato verses to inform
The world of my perceptions.
Running out of time standing here
Sitting here
I search for elongated stanzas
Characters to better tell tales
Of this great vanishing act which becomes me
As it was me
And shall be me;
Because it was before me.
Not enough momentum
Even the trains seem slower
With a caution based in lawsuits
And mass spiritual gentrification
Or was that pacification of the mind of this place
Every place in the sunset so far as I can tell.
And Chris drew a picture in school today
One he hoped would make his father cry
A picture of himself with a gun in his hand
Standing by a mass of people with no eyes...
Cartoon characters make easier truths
Of souls running with no life
Than delayed tracks
Inaudible announcements
And too much trash lost from situations that aren't right.
There never seems to be enough time anymore
Looking for answers on faces which speak far too similar
A beige world of existence
I long for colors I cannot comprehend
And a taste upon my tongue
Only the devil could defend...

-State of Awareness-

Because my sunrise dims faster every day
Because my heart outweighs my pay
And I know I'll lose
more than I will save
Because she got the better deal
Purse instead of steel
And afterthought's become my mantra;
Because my people are my people
Relegated consumerist
And my government needed a system
And nobody else would be havin' it;
Because I'm not a hero to my students
And won't be a victim for my politicians
Numbers are best for dollar bills
Because the alternative would be chaos
But maybe that's God's will
Because my heart can't take it
Never knowing the origin of blood it pumps
I am forever a shadow
Across the hues of this and other lands;
And murder is just a shout away.
Because I enjoy the morning most
Blessed surprise
Every day a birth day
Renewed chance to hone my goals
To make my dreams a reality;
Sprig's vibrancy coupled with morning's dew,
And you?

Because she stares a little more each day
Wants a moment more each time
Despite my attempts to drown
within my mind
Curious about her curiosity
As it makes for another line.
Because it is now, as it was then
Consistently inconsistence
becomes my survival
Looking for new paths
off the trail man's planned for me;
And I can witness it upon their faces
Every day inching closer to a world
Ready to masticate their being
Swallow their souls
Ingesting the nutrients of promises
To defecate what remains upon a plate
for their spawn to ingest...

Because I work in reality
One stop away from the line's end
Unless transfer is made
To an express opposite direction of the mind
And I am tired, too tired
So tired;
And the dew won't survive the morning.

And you?

-Enough-

I think they want us all angry.
Systematically our heroes
Made negative
Our music
Made negative
Our appearance
Made negative
Our collective soul now
Born negative.
Somewhere
Some people got together and said
'Enough!'
'These niggers
have learned how to play OUR
game, and lessons need to be taught.'
Somewhere
Some people got the idea
That we will let them kill each other,
So that way,
When we do it...
NO INDICTMENT.
PROBABLE CAUSE.
EXCESSIVE FORCE.
NECESSARY.
And what the fuck are they gonna do?
Then someone answered,
'Eventually, they'll all get angry.
No matter their station, their mind,
no matter their God,
no matter their dime.

Enough
Will be enough
And we will have them right
Where we want them.'
My parents
My blood
My God
Said be a good man
Work hard and respect
But in this land,
What is the use
When as it provideth
It surely doth taketh away
Not because it needs to,
But it wants to.

I want this place to burn.
I want to see my friends
Burn
Want to see my enemies
Burn
I want to smell this city
Burn
I want to feast upon the charred flesh
of the remnants of war
and make sure my captors know
Enough
Is
ENOUGH...

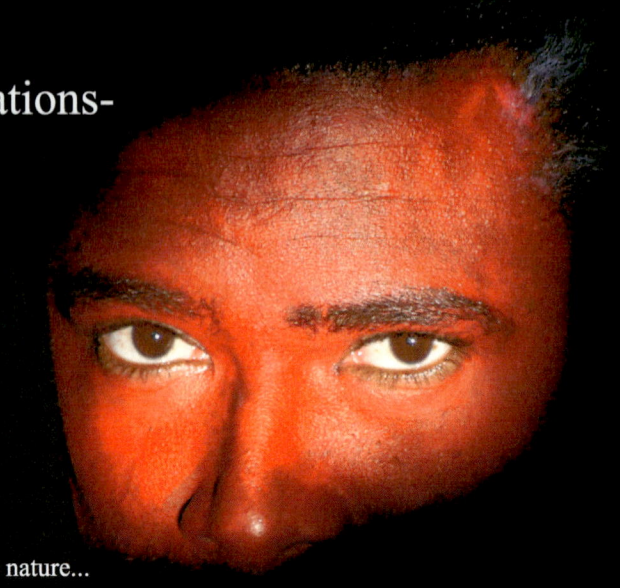

-Pompeii Conversations-

On and on you go
Your lips exercising about.
You make a few good points
Cause me to think for a moment
But you won't shut up...
I need a moment of silence
To take things in
Dissect the abundant characters
Spewing from your Vesuvius
You so eloquently informed me
Erupts due to your uncomfortable nature...
Just a moment
To be sure
I'm not listening to a recording
To remind myself
That at some point
I found something
Anything
Intriguing about you
And there is more to you
As our Pompeii
Slowly
Methodically
Drowns in your molten wake.

-Catch 22-

Caught in a catch-22
Damned if I don't
Beyond fucked if I do.
Already dressed in black skin
Mind
Whatever form of covering I choose for today
I make like Johnny Cash
Walk the line
Teetering on salvation and destruction,
Or is it the other way around?
Caught in a catch-22
Roses are best in red
And my songs seem beset in blue
Notes floating effortlessly
Somewhere in between a plea for help
And a roar of anger
Because no matter what I say in this moment
I'm dammed if I do
Already ass-up faced down 'cause I don't
Want a war;
Senseless head-slamming against walls
Solidified
Petrified with age.
Caught in your catch-22
History enslaves me
But you hold the keys to freedom
Ours
Merrily
Variably I say unto thee
You and I are a chorus
Singing only because we are caged
Now tethered to
Entwined
You lost you, and I gave up me
Though I catch-22 attempt to hold on...
Loosely
And my blindness allows me to see,
I'm dammed if I'm you
And FUCKED for being me!

-Stage 2-

4am on a Thursday morning
And now you move on to stage 2.
Fate and sickness interrupted my dreams
Caused me to pick up my brilliant playground and wander;
Or so I thought,
Because moments later, there you were signaling me
Strumming my conscious with your need acceptable
For an explanation of events
You think you are ready to hear.
As with step one,
I understand.
It's just the process of things
Evolution of the heart and mind's workings
Still ultimately as mysterious as death;
Finality,
Conclusion,
Words which now and
Forever,
Will reverberate an entirety of new meanings
Within your mind
Because I was number one...
In this one way,
And could never be,
Should never be,
But so need to be
In every other.

Selfish?
Think on it a while.
Correlate
Connect the dots of yesterdays and tomorrows
And as I have so often
So shall you too understand every pieces placement
Movement
Upon this chess set we've named existence.
I know,
It's not what you want to hear right now
What you will never want to hear...
But this is stage 2
And nothing I divulge at this time will matter
Despite your thinking it would.
Now there's only the simmer of time
As you've turned things over and over in sorrow and
hurt
And are just waiting for this course to be done;
The dishes which leave the best taste take time
And there are many more to flow.

-Linger-

I don't want it to linger
I don't want it to bruise
But you point your finger
And in the end we both lose
I don't want you to sing me
Songs that confuse
About how you want me
As I am but with rules
I don't want it to linger
I just want it to end
Let's just get past the drama
Maybe we could be friends
I don't want it to linger
With my heart on the mend
But you touch me softly
And I'm back in your sin
I don't want it to linger
I don't want it to bruise
But love is forever
Even with all that we lose
I don't want it to linger
Without you I'll choose
I don't want you to bring me
Flowers that ruse
Songs sweet from your lips
That seek to abuse
In my fragile state of mind
Thinking you kind
I'm likely to fall
Though I'd lose it all...

-Without Words-

Without words I sing
Call you to come
Rest here upon mine heart
Beating now only for you.
Without words I dream
Make due until your arms can still me
Rest me from the movement of this hunt
Inescapable for a better song to sing
Like these birds in flight above me
Freedom works best with wings.
Without words I love you
Want to
Every day you
The smile you bring to my weary truth
Ignition to this slowing mind
As it tries not to petrify in age;
You
Renew
Without words
Undo the coils of my existence
Send my walls to ruin
Setting my secrets free
Leaving only a lifetime to spend with you
Without words
Only peace.

-Goodbyes Going-

Connection again
I am charged
Rejuvenated
with the elixir of possibility
Of tasting
Holding
Knowing you in ways
I thought had vanished
As days slipped into weeks
Ran quicker still to months
Which flew on to become years.
Connection again
I no longer wait on my heart's
proverbial line for a human voice
to answer my multitude of questions
of questions
about the already far too many questions
I've asked as I pondered you
In the lines of another story
As I scripted yet another verse
in preparation of this moment here with you now.
Now I stare again profoundly into you
Watch you tumbling over reality and wants
On to resolution that
This
Is us
and that all we have is now
along with the burden of goodbye
Again, and those promises uttered
just to keep the heart going
Pulse going
Dream going
Goodbyes
Going...

~The Beast Within~

In my latest dream
There was devour
Predator to the prey
We didn't get real far
Which one of them was me?
2nd dream
Which would be you?
No shelter near
Camouflaged
I think I've soured on the taste of you
And yet I pursue
Driver grasping this wheel
Attempting to traverses this pain blinding...
I need to grow up
Stop looking for those jewels in the rain
Steady downpour of truth and loneliness
Hiding behind my pursuit of freedom;
I fear I'm drowning.
Diamonds in the rainbow
Add a sparkle to the struggle
A sparkle to the art
Created of the pressures of this existence.
Can you find the time to listen?
Mind you find the time to learn?
I am but an answer to some form of equation
To barely seeing the heat
As I'm caught
Within society's infinitesimal eyes
Making it impossible to sense anything but the night
Hold on;
Gone
This thing haunting
With every turn in the road of existence.
Wraith of my conscious
Holds on
Dead eyes set
Slowly and deliberately...
To number one
Beginning endlessly this journey
To the depths of me
And as always,
The destruction I crave so.

Rogerio Bussad :

Brazilian at birth and New Yorker at heart, he is a self taught intuitive photographer. With a passion and dedication to the photogenic arts, he primarily explores still life, B&W, Portraiture, and the use of unexpected elements as models and/or inspiration. With 'Elemental', he seeks to expand and push his creative endeavors into a new realm and audience. He states, 'Inspiration comes in many forms and at different times. I enjoy focusing on the ordinary aspects of daily life that we sometimes take for granted. My work evolves naturally, organically combining whatever element which sparks the creativity and my vision. Fond as I am of telling a story through an image, I try to touch the viewer and evoke emotions, so that they can create their own stories based on my photography.' Learn and see more of his work via

Facebook - Rogerio Bussad Photography

Tim Stachecki :

Based in Northport, LI, he is a self-defined artist who works in multiple medias including photography, paint, ceramics, sculpture, and the written word. He has performed and produced his art for audiences and collectors from coast to coast and celebrates his eleventh anniversary as a freelance artist this year.
You can view some of his work via www.tsdesignlab.com

or via Facebook - Tim Stachecki's Studio